POPPER

15 EASY STUDIES
Preparatory to Studies Opus 76 & 73

FOR CELLO
(with Cello II ad libitum)

(G. WOERL)

Published in 2019 by Allegro Editions

15 Easy Studies for Two Cellos
ISBN: 978-1-9748-9969-2 (paperback)

Cover design by Kaitlyn Whitaker

Cover image: "Cello" by Mindscape Studio, courtesy of Shutterstock;
"Music Sheet" by danielo, courtesy of Shutterstock

ALLEGRO EDITIONS

15 EASY STUDIES
Preparatory to Studies Opus 76 & 73

1.

Edited by G. WOERL

DAVID POPPER
(1843-1913)

2.

Con moto *(alla marcia)*

3.

Allegretto

5.

Allegro vivace

6.

7.

15

17

11.

Allegro molto vivace

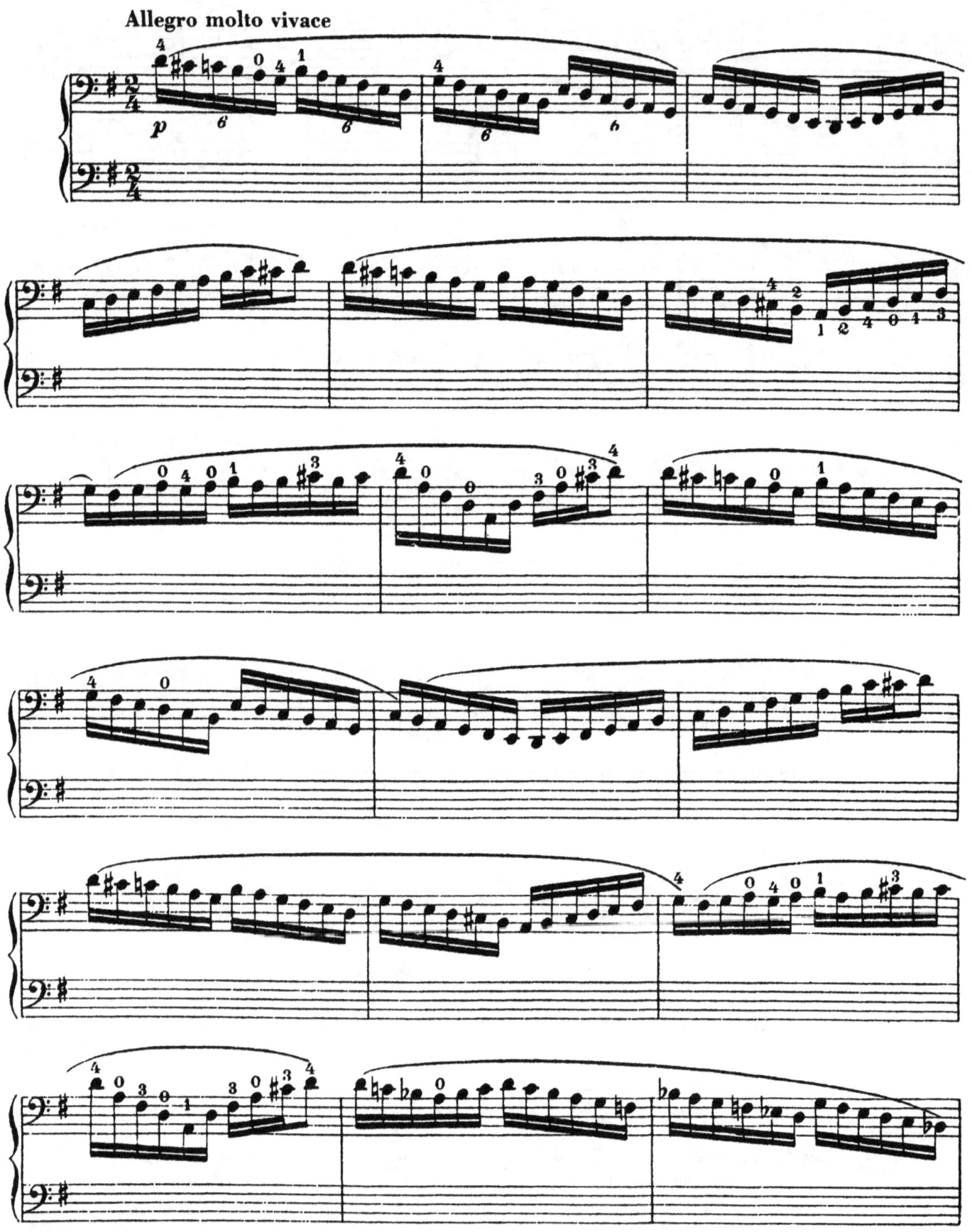

A second Cello part was not composed for this study.

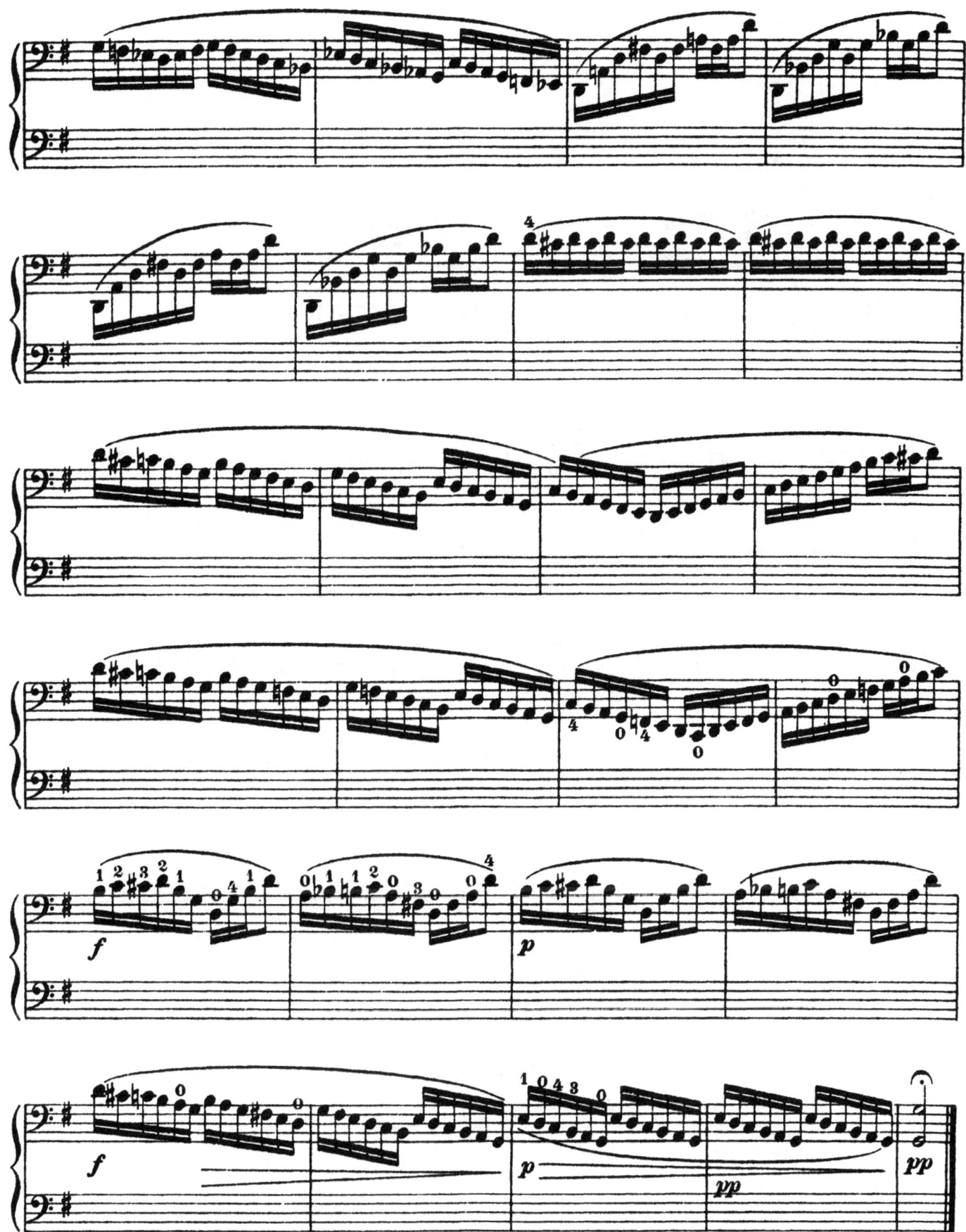

12.

MINUET
Moderato

A second Cello part was not composed for this study.

13.

A second Cello part was not composed for this study.

14.

A second Cello part was not composed for this study.

25

15.

A second Cello part was not composed for this study.

27

www.ingramcontent.com/pod-product-compliance
Lightning Source LLC
LaVergne TN
LVHW061344060426
835512LV00016B/2665